It is Finished

By

Dr. Anthony Spero

ISBN: 1-931178-63-1

Vision Publishing
1520 Main St. C
Ramona, CA 92065
www.visionpublishingservices.com

Scriptures taken from the New American Standard Bible
and the New International Version
unless otherwise stated.

Dedication

I affectionately dedicate this book to my wife, Mary, who has been a source of strength and encouragement in my ministry.

Table of Contents

Forward

Due to the recent theatrical release of the Mel Gibson movie *The Passion of the Christ*, much has been written and discussed on the suffering of Christ for all mankind on the cross. This one historical event has change life on earth for all eternity, and every true believer is forever grateful for what Christ has done for us through his suffering.

As important as the passion is as a historical event, its meaning is much more significant. On Calvary's' tree our sins were paid for, and entrance to eternal life was made available for all. Through Christ sacrifice, Christians throughout all ages have entered into a covenant relationship with God, purchased by the precious blood of our savior, and has opened to us blessing upon blessing by His wonderful grace and mercy.

As we have pondered (for those who have chosen to watch the Passion) the death of Christ through the abhorrent instrument of the cross, many have also considered in great depth the life of we have received in Him. Not only quantity of life, but quality, in terms of the many benefits Christ has been purchased for us. Yet, and sadly so often truly, many believers live as though the life of Christ poured out for us was merely for entrance into heaven (it certainly is that) and does not provide the abundant life here as Christ promised (John 10:10). Rather than abundance, many live far below their inheritance, in spite of their many prayers and confessions to the contrary. Why do believers live beneath their means in God? It is to address this very problem, the problem of the average believer living only an average life instead of the abundant life of joyful fulfillment Christ has promised that this excellent book by Dr. Spero has been written.

What did Jesus mean when he stated emphatically with his last breath "It is finished"? Was it resignation, life was over, His purpose fulfilled? Was it relief that death had come and now He could return to his Father? Perhaps some or even all of this is true. But perhaps even more importantly, His statement on the cross can be seen as a proclamation. To the principalities and powers, to the Jewish leaders, to friend and foe, disciple and detractor, His resounding proclamation was that all that was wrong was now being made right, all injustice made just, all fear trumped by love, all death swallowed up in victory. It is finished! No more powerful and wonderful words were ever spoken. For in these words are the hopes for all mankind. Finished is separation from a loving and holy God, finished was the triumph of fear over faith, finished was the dominion of Satan, sickness, disease and lack in the life of the believer. Finally, the ability to live life as God intended was now possible, and became the birth right of every Christian. It is now the responsibility of the Spirit enlivened believer to live the life Christ has given. To do so requires obedience, faith, courage, and a clear understanding of the Word of God, and the willingness to apply the principles of the Word to our daily experience.

I am grateful that my friend and fellow minister to many nations, Anthony Spero has written this most balanced and life affirming book on the important of the work of Christ on the Cross. It will change the life of any reader who will take serious the concepts and apply them judiciously to their life in Christ.

Stan DeKoven, Ph.D.
President
Vision International College and University

Author's Forward

It only seems like yesterday that I graduated from Zion Bible Institute and launched into a life of ministry. My wife and I were filled with optimism, believing our life was destined for true greatness. Well, nearly 42 years later, I look back on things great and small, evangelistic campaigns, churches planted, missions in Africa and India, training leaders for the harvest field. Though these many years, and the trials of church life, my faith in the goodness and grace of God has been the most sustaining aspect of our life in God.

Faith is a much-maligned topic of late. Sadly, many have seen faith as a magic formula to manipulate God for new cars and better jobs. Though I certainly believe God intends to bless his children because he loves us and desires to bless us, there is always a purpose behind the blessing…that we might fulfill the covenant of God.

We must remember that faith is not a minor theme of the Word of God, but a vital part of our life. By faith the worlds were formed, by faith nations are transformed by the gospel, through faith we have received life by grace, and without faith, pleasing God is impossible.

The life of a Christian is a journey of faith. Having walked this life of faith, I look back with joy at the goodness of God. But even more so do I look forward to fulfilling greater feats of faith, based upon the finished work of Christ on the cross, and to eventually enjoy for eternity the rewards of God's grace appropriated by faith.

Why Another Book on Faith?

I asked the Lord on more than one occasion, why should I write on this topic? First, I do not deem myself for a moment gifted in writing (speaking is hard enough for this Boston born and bred preacher). Further, I have but a few stories of triumphant faith, great miracles, and abundant prosperity that others more qualified have experienced and written about. Yet, I suppose I do have a perspective, a belief that there is room for a fresh look at this most important subject, presented with (hopefully) balance and conviction.

Many Christians struggle with biblically settled issues. Our salvation was provided for us through the cross of Christ…we need not struggle but receive Christ's provision by faith. Our sanctification (being set aside for God and made clean by Christ's blood) is provided for (of course, it must be appropriated by faith).

Healing has been provided for by the atoning work of Christ on the cross (by his stripes, we were healed, 1 Pet. 2:24), and can be appropriated by faith. Even our prosperity, when understood biblically can be appropriated by faith, and has been provided for us by the finished work of Christ on the cross.

It is finished. But what has Christ finished for us, what does it mean for you, and how do we appropriate it?

This is the purpose for this book. To help you to appropriate by faith all the promises of God, for they are yours, they are mine; for our journey. Christ has finished the work of our full and complete redemption "It is Finished"- so let's begin.

Deuteronomy 30:19

"I call heaven and earth to record this day against you, that I have set before you life and death, blessing and cursing: therefore choose life."

Chapter I

The Essential Importance of Faith

There are many books written today about what God has already provided for us as Christians through the finished work of Jesus on Calvary's Cross. Each one of the writers of these books list the common denominator for one experiencing the benefits of what Christ has already provided for mankind is; faith. That is true. The bible plainly tells us from cover to cover that faith in God is the most essential element one needs to manifest and release into ones life the things that Christ has provided for them as Christians. Why is this so? Because when one chooses to place ones faith in God what one is actually doing is giving to God the right and authority to intervene in the affairs of life. Ones lack of faith in God only serves to hinder God from becoming intimately involved in the affairs of life. Let me explain this.

In Genesis 1:26 Moses writes, "So God created man in His own image and in His likeness giving to him dominion over the fish of the sea, over the birds of the air, over the cattle, over all the earth and over every creeping thing that creeps on the earth." What is Moses saying to us in this verse? He is telling us the parameters by which God governs His relationship with man. It is very important for us as Christians to understand what is meant by parameters and how they affect us as believers. God is the one who has set these parameters in His word. What Moses is telling us is God has in His sovereignty determined that each of us as human beings have the authority over our own lives. Because He has done this, it limits what He is able to do for us (again, by God's choice, a part of His marvelous plan for us). He is only able to do for us what we give Him access to do. We have legal authority to choose what degree we will allow Him to do what He wills to do for us. We exercise the authority given to us by the measure of faith we place in Him. If we have no faith in Him He is limited (by design) when it comes to the Lord having the authority to do what He wills to do for us. If we have great faith, we take the shackles off our lack of faith placed on His hands and allow Him the freedom to bless us with all the provisions Christ has already provided for us. The measure of faith we display in life determines the degree God is able to accomplish what He wills to accomplish in our lives. Faith in God is the vehicle that determines what access we will allow God to have in the affairs of our life.

It is important as Christians that we understand one particular truth about God. Though his ways are above our ways, in some respects He is like every one of us as human beings, in that He is governed by His word. He will not violate the principles of His word. He has already established in His word the principles to govern both Himself and mankind. Whether we realize it or not, God is governed by the same word that governs our lives. His Word is not only law for mankind but it is the same law He is governed by. God is committed to His word that even though He may want to do something for us, He will not violate His word. This bible tells us that He places His word equal with His own name. (Ps. 138:2)

God set the boundaries of how He would govern the affairs of this universe in creation. In setting these boundaries God relinquished His rights to do what He wills to do in each of our lives. If that were not true then all men would be saved. Why? Because it is His will that all man be saved. However, because God chose to relinquish some of His rights to do what He wills to do, He will not intervene in the affairs of life until we give Him the authority to do so. We can only give Him that right through inviting Him into the situation we want Him to get involved, and we do so by faith.

Again, notice what Moses tells us in Genesis 1:26. God gave dominion to man only over lower creation, not man, including himself; that dominion belongs to God solely. He did give to man the gift of freedom of choice! He tells us at creation God gave to man dominion over the affairs of his person life. In doing this, and in order for God to be able to release all the benefits that Christ has provided for mankind, man must first of all give God the legal authority to do so. Of course, as believers we gave the Lord legal authority over our lives when we accepted Christ as savior and Lord. If a man or woman does not receive Christ, thus giving to God the legal authority to release Christ finished work in his life, God would be guilty of unlawful intrusion into a persons life. God will not do that. That is why faith plays such an important role in God's work for us. According to the boundaries set by God in creation, faith is the key element that allows God the freedom to intervene in the affairs of man. In other words, faith is like a vehicle that takes man to the destination he wants to go. When man places his faith in God, faith in God becomes the vehicle that gives God full access into ones life, allowing God to accomplish what He wills to accomplish in that persons life. When we fail to put our faith in God what we are really doing is choosing not to give God full authority to do what he wills to do for us as Christians. That is why the writer of Hebrews tells us that the will of God for us is to provide to us things that please Him. What are the things that please God? Releasing into our lives the very things that His son Jesus Christ has already provided for us through His death and resurrection.

Let's go one step further. Why does faith in God give God the authority to operate in ones life. In Genesis 12 we find the account of the beginning of events that transpired in the life of the patriarch Abraham. After the fall of man God desired a man who would give Him access into the lives of all people. God has the ability to do all things, and there is nothing impossible with Him, yet He purposely limited Himself to what He is willing to do in the affairs of mankind, giving to man the key whereby He could once again become fully engaged in the affairs of man's life. When God called Abram in Genesis 12 God was giving to him the opportunity to be the door whereby God could once again have the authority to accomplish in the lives of mankind the things that God desired to accomplish for them. One thing that can be learned both from this story and other stories from the bible is every action God takes here on earth requires the involvement of a human being, by God's design. That is why when God needed access into the lives of people, Moses tells us in Genesis 12 God called to Himself a man named Abram. Abram became the vehicle for God to have full access to accomplish what He desired too here on earth.

What is God's ultimate desire? What is His involvement in the affairs of man? The answer is simple. It is to bless mankind by making him all that He created them to be, thus providing man with everything that man would ever need in life in order for man to live a favored and successful life.

However, before God could accomplish His purpose He needed to have access into the hearts of man. Thus God called Abram, giving him the opportunity to choose whether or not he would be His instrument, giving Him access into the affairs of man. Notice the words God spoke to Abram, whose name was later changed to Abraham, in verse 1 of Genesis 12.

"Get out of your country and go to the land I will show you." "I will make you a great nation and I will bless you and through you all the nations of the earth will be blessed."

In order for God to become involved with meeting the needs of mankind He chose Abraham to work His will through. God told Abraham I will make of your seed a great nation. Notice the reason why God wanted to make Abraham seed a great nation. So that all the nations of the earth would be blessed. Thus all nations could enjoy the benefits of what Jesus Christ had already provided before the foundations of the earth. But in order for this to happen Abraham had to do what God told Him to do. Why? Because Abraham's act of obedience was an act of faith. Abraham's act of faith would give to God access into his life, and through obedience, Abraham's seed and the rest of the nations of the world were/are blessed. Obedience to God's word is a manifestation of ones faith in God. When Abraham obeyed God by doing what God told him to do, not only his life but the lives of his family members and every single one of us who would ever live here on planet earth we blessed. Abraham's act of faith allowed God the

right to accomplish the very things He wants to do for man today. What was the motivating factor for Abraham to do what God told him to do? He believed what God said to him. Thus, faith became the vehicle that motivated Abraham to give to God the access to intervene in the affairs of mankind. That same faith was the very thing that allowed God to release both to Abraham and his family all the blessing of God's provisions.

Powerful Progressive Purpose

Notice the progression of the purpose of God's call in Abraham's life. God called Abraham to be the father of a great nation. That nation God called Abraham to father is the nation of Israel. What was God's purpose in establishing the nation of Israel? That all the nations of the earth would be blessed through her, that all the nations of the earth could experience the benefits of God's provision. God's purpose in calling Abraham wasn't just to bless him and his family but that God would have access through them to the whole human race, whereby through them He could bless all the nations of the earth. God called Abraham to be an instrument He could use whereby all the nations of the earth could be blessed.

Herein lays the ultimate purpose of ones faith in God. Faith in God is not a magical tool intended by God to bless and make us prosperous. This is one of the results of faith in God. But it is God's desire to bless us and make us a blessing to the world we live in. Once we give God access our lives God is then able to release to us all the benefits Christ has provided for, making us an instrument to bless those people around us, establishing His Kingdom here on earth as it is in heaven.

What God's word points out to us is faith in God does not only release all the benefits Christ has provided for us, but is also the vehicle God uses to make us an instrument to release the very same blessing God has blessed us with to others. Faith in God is not just about what we can get from God, but it is God's method how He, through us, can have access into the life of others, so he can bless others through us. Sadly, many Christians have missed the purpose for having faith in God. Remember, faith in God isn't a vehicle to just bless us; it is a gift we use to give God full access into our lives as a blessing to others through us. Abraham's' faith in God released God's authority into Abraham's life whereby God could make him a father of a great nation. Through that nation all nations of the earth became blessed.

As you read this book that it will challenge you to allow God to have complete access into your life, so you can reap the benefits of all that Christ has provided. It will I trust, further challenge you to be the seed of Abraham today.

This book is intended to be God's voice to you today, reminding you that many have lived a life of either selfish or simply non-appropriated faith long enough. It is time for us to repent and recognize the true purpose of faith in God and possess the land Christ has provided for us. Giving God access, not only into ones life, but also to those around us is essential. Such faith will not only release Christ finished work in us but will also release God's purpose in the lives we touch.

II Peter 1: 3

"According to His divine power He has given unto us all things pertaining to life and godliness."

Chapter II

Knowing What is Rightfully Ours in Christ Jesus

Do you, as a born again believer, know what is rightfully yours in Christ Jesus? Or are you like many Christians today who can be likened to the Israelites of old, walking circles in the desert, wandering in a wilderness, disturbed and confused, when God has so much more for your life?

When God delivered Israel out of Egyptian captivity, it was His will for them to enjoy complete redemption by possessing the land of Canaan. It was never God's intention for Israel to wander in the wilderness for 40 years. Israel brought this upon themselves because they lacked the faith to obey God's word, march in and possess the land when they came to Canaan's borders. Israel's unbelief robbed them of their rightful inheritance. God had provided complete deliverance for all of the Israelites who left Egypt, yet only Joshua and Caleb and everyone twenty years old and younger would be the ones who would enjoy what God had provided.

Perhaps, like so many Christians today, you may be in an all-too-common place of disappointment in your walk with God. You have accepted Jesus Christ as your Savior, but because it hasn't been all you anticipated it would be, you are sometimes more disappointed in your experience than excited about it. Theoretically, you know Christ is the only answer to your problems. Yet, it seems your problems are expanding instead of being resolved. Your problem is not that God has failed to fulfill His promises to you, but may be caused by your inability (often due to no fault of your own) to appropriate complete redemption for yourself. Perhaps you have lacked the faith or a clear understanding

of just how to "possess your possessions" (Obadiah 17), to lay hold of what is rightfully yours. You have been satisfied with just a partial redemption, often without realizing it, when Christ has provided you with complete redemption.
Jesus said in Matthew 11:28-30,

> *"Come unto me, all ye that labor and are heavy laden, and I will give you rest. Take my yoke upon you, and learn of me; for I am meek and lowly in heart; and ye shall find rest unto your souls. For my yoke is easy, and my burden is light."*

The key words in this portion of scripture are "learn of me". One of the important truths Jesus is communicating is that if you want rest, strength, power and peace, then "learn of me". (Isa. 30:15) This is not a new problem…It has been a problem for believers since time began.

It is time for you, as a child of God, to understand the full meaning and power of your redemption. Once you do, you will know the full blessings of your inheritance, as Christ, captivates your life and you realize Christianity isn't a religion, but a way of life under the control of a living God.

One of the last statements Jesus made on Calvary's cross before He died is recorded in John 19:30, where He stated "It is finished". Jesus, in this proclamation, was telling all humanity that the full work of redemption has been completed. Every provision we need to live this present life in its fullest sense has been provided for us through the atonement.[1] All we need do is accept by faith all the

---

[1] "The redeeming of mankind and the reconciliation of God with man, brought about by Jesus' sufferings and death." (New World Dictionary, 1988)

benefits Christ provided for us. Too often theologians declare that Christ died just for the salvation of our souls. Be satisfied knowing your sins are forgiven and you are on your way to heaven. But that is just part of your redemption. Christ's death and resurrection was for the whole man; your body, soul, and spirit. Paul's benediction to the church in Thessalonica gives us a picture of God's plan.

> *"Now may the God of peace Himself sanctify you entirely; and may your spirit, and soul and body be preserved complete without blame at the coming of our Lord Jesus Christ". (I Thessalonians 5:23)*

The sooner we realize God's plan and accept it by faith, the sooner Christianity will become a way of life for us, instead of a dull, boring religion.

Satan will do everything in his power to keep Christians ignorant of what Jesus has provided for them. He knows once Christians possess what is rightfully theirs in Christ Jesus, they will not let him push them around any longer, but they will use their God-given authority over him. Jesus said in Matthew 28:18,

> *"All power is given unto me in heaven and in earth."*

Since we, as Christians, are in Christ Jesus, this power that has been given to Jesus has been delegated to us. Paul points out the reality of this truth in Colossians 2:9, 10.

> *"For in Him dwells all the fullness of the God head in bodily form. And you are*

complete in Him, which is the head of all principality and power."

The Word of God likens a Christian's relationship to Christ to the functioning of the physical body. Believers compose the body of Christ, while Jesus is the Head of the body. In our physical body our head, the lodging place of our brain, controls the movements of the rest of our body. Our brain delegates the power for our legs to walk, or our hands to move, and our various organs to function. We would be powerless if our brain failed to do its job. As our physical head is the most vital member of our physical being, our spiritual head, Jesus Christ, is the most vital member in the spiritual body. He is the source of all the strength and power we need. As we trust in Him, He controls our lives, and we are complete in Him.

As Christians, it is very important for us to possess our completeness, which Christ has provided for us, by faith (Obadiah 17). For in so doing, we are walking in the truth. Jesus said in John 8:32,

"And ye shall know the truth, and the truth shall make you free..."

The truth causes us to see that we are free, delivered from Satan's shackles. Therefore, we are not under the dominion of sin any longer. That is true liberty, and wonderfully good news!

Paul, who lived in the reality of complete redemption, knew the truth. He refused to live under the shackles of sin. That is why he could state with great assurance in Romans 6:14,

"For sin shall not have dominion over you: for ye are not under the law, but under grace,"

God's grace is the very means by which Christian are provided complete redemption, full wholeness.

Once we have accepted God's grace, which sets us free from the dominion of sin, we must continue to possess our inheritance by faith. Paul points this out clearly in Galatians 5:1 when he writes,

"Stand fast therefore in the liberty wherewith Christ hath made us free, and be not entangled again with the yoke of bondage."

Paul, in different words, but meaning the same thing, was saying to the Galatians what God told Israel in Deuteronomy 1:8 – to possess the land He had set before them. God provided Israel with the land, but in order for them to enjoy it, they still had to go in and possess it.

God has provided us liberty from sin, sickness and poverty through Jesus Christ. All we have to do is possess it by standing fast in what is ours. If you fail to possess what is yours in Christ Jesus, you cannot enjoy salvation in its fullest sense, and Satan will have been successful in robbing you of Christ's best for your life.

In John 10:10, Jesus tells us that Satan is out to rob us of what Christ has provided for us.

"The thief comes not, but for to steal, and to kill, and to destroy: I am come that they

might have life, and that they might have it more abundantly."

The abundant life is a victorious life; life in its fullest sense. The abundant life knows no defeat, for its strength comes from God. It is not without life's struggles, but as Paul states in Romans 8:37, it is an overcoming life.

"But in all these things we overwhelmingly conquer through Him who loved us."

In what things are we more than conquerors? In all things pertaining to life and godliness we conquer. For in Christ there is nothing that can separate us from our rightful heritage.

Finally, Paul says in Romans 8:35,

"Who shall separate us from the love of Christ? Shall tribulation, or distress, or persecution, or famine, or nakedness, or peril, or sword?"

No, nothing can separate us from our liberty in Christ. When trouble, problems, financial needs, disaster, sickness or death come knocking at our door, remember that Christ has provided for us deliverance in the midst of such circumstances, and they cannot defeat us.

"God wants to take us from a place of little habitation to a place of habitation." Exodus 15:13

"They wandered in the wilderness in a solitary place (little habitation)." Psalms 107:4

"And He led them forth by the right way, to a city of habitation." Psalms 107:7

Chapter III

You Have Stayed Here Long Enough

The Lord God spoke to Israel at Mt. Horeb and said,

> *"You have stayed here on this mountain long enough." (Deuteronomy 1:6).*

In this passage, Moses the great leader of the children of Israel begins to rehearse to the Children of Israel their 40 year journey in the wilderness. It had been 40 years since God first spoke these words, (See Numbers 13 and14) commanding the people to possess their possessions. Sadly, they refused to obey God, and the results were disastrous.

After God manifested Himself in a mighty way by delivering Israel out of the hands of the Egyptians, He led them by a cloud in the daytime and a pillar of fire by night to Mt. Horeb. It was there at Mt. Horeb that God revealed His presence to Israel by speaking to the Israelites in an audible voice. Further, it was at Mt. Horeb that God gave Israel the Ten Commandments and other laws to help guide their lives.

Israel was content to live in the shadows of Mt. Horeb, for it was there that the Israelites enjoyed God's Protection from their enemies and manna (food) from heaven. To coin a modern day expression, the Israelites "had a good thing going." Even though Israel was enjoying all of these benefits, her people were only enjoying a portion of what God had in store for them.

Israel would have been satisfied to continue to live by Mt. Horeb and never fulfill their purpose in God, if God would have allowed the Israelites to do so. God declared that it was time to pack up their tents and move on. He had much more in store for them in Canaan's land than they could ever receive at Mt. Horeb.

After God told the Israelites they had dwelt at Mt. Horeb long enough, he told them He had provided Canaan's land for them and that all they had to do was march in and possess it. "Behold, I have set the land before you, go in and possess the land." (Deuteronomy 1:8). In that same verse, God gave Israel the instructions on how to possess the land. He said they should possess it boldly, without fear or discouragement. Why? Because He had already provided it for them. Since the land belonged to them, all they had to do was obey God's command and possess it. Sure, they would face obstacles, but there weren't any obstacles to fear or to become discouraged about, because God would give them the victory over all of them.

Many Christians today are like the Israelites of Old. They are satisfied being saved, content to be on their way to heaven. They have no desire to enter into the fullness of their salvation. They are satisfied being babes in Christ, drinking the milk of God's Word, when God has provided a T-bone steak for them. Such Christians fear launching out into the deep, preferring to walk by sight and feelings, instead of living by faith in God's Word. They want to see the end at the beginning, instead of trusting in the leadership of Christ, believing He knows what is best for them.

Solomon tells us in Proverbs 3:5-6,

> *"Trust in the Lord with all your heart, and lean not on your own understanding. In all*

your ways acknowledge him, and he shall direct your path."

Christians find it hard to simply trust God. We prefer to trust in our own understanding, which usually creates problems. Our natural understanding teaches us to rationalize God's Word instead of acting upon it by faith. Because Christians rely on their understanding more than the Word of God, their understanding becomes the very factor that robs them of their heritage in Christ Jesus.

When we, as born again believers, manifest faith in God's Word by acting upon it, our faith becomes the factor that releases God to honor His Word. It is time for Christians to realize that faith in God's Word is the key that opens the vault of heaven's treasury.

As we read the Bible, we will notice one important fact. Whenever a man or woman acted upon God's Word in faith, God responded to their faith by fulfilling His Word on their behalf. Faith in God's Word was the very motivation that caused Abraham to leave his country and family and go to the land God had directed him to go to. God told Abraham in Genesis 12:2, 3 that if he would have the faith to act upon His Word, He would bless him and make of him a great nation.

If Abraham would have rationalized God's Word away instead of acting upon it, he would have missed out on the blessing of God. Abraham, by faith, obeyed God's Word and left his country. God, in turn, blessed him and made Abraham's seed a great nation. Both the Jewish and Arab peoples today are a testimony of Abrahams' faith in God's Word and God's blessing upon Abraham.

If you are a Christian who has been satisfied with just a partial redemption, God is speaking to you today as He spoke to Israel at Mt. Horeb, "you have lived here long enough." It is time for you to launch out in faith in His provisions, and possess your complete redemption.

God told Israel to launch out and possess her inheritance boldly. The Word of God is proclaiming the very same message to Christians today. Possess your inheritance, which has been provided for you, with boldness, and without fear or discouragement.

Many Christians have said that they would like to possess everything Christ has provided for them, but they don't dare because every time they try to appropriate God's Word, their problems increase. This may happen, but remember that it is only Satan trying to discourage and rob you of something precious which Christ has provided. Satan doesn't want you to enter into complete redemption because he realizes once you do, you will then use the authority Christ has provided for you, making you a powerful enemy of Satan's plans. That is why he will do everything in his power to discourage you from manifesting the faith you need to possess your rightful inheritance in Christ.

You must always remember that the closer you line to the Lord, the more you will realize your authority him Him. You can overcome any problem through Him. John writes in 1 John 4:4,

> *"Greater is He that is in you, than he that is in the world."*

They Failed to Enter

As the story goes, the children of Israel, like so many individual believers and even churches, failed to enter into the promise. It was, and always will be, God's will to enter the rest of God. In Christ, we enter His rest, but the Kingdom of God, which we enter when we are born again, requires possession. Let's see what hindered the people of God then and can hinder God's people today.

"And the Lord said unto Joshua, **<u>see</u>** I have given unto your hand the Jericho (the city). Joshua 6: 2

Chapter IV

Let Us Go Up and Possess the Land

When God speaks to us through His Word, He expects us to respond by acting upon His Word without adding stipulations to it. If we obey His Word, we will enjoy the blessings of God. If we fail to obey God's Word, we will hinder God's plan from being fulfilled in our lives. The results of disobedience include confusion, frustration, and many other potential problems.

As children of God, we should delight in obeying the Word of God. For God hasn't given us His Word to rob us from enjoying life. He has given us His Word as a means to guide us in finding life in its fullness.

As stated in the last chapter, God told the Israelites to go in and possess the land He provided for them. In Deuteronomy 1:22, Moses again reminds the people of the fatal mistake of the now perished generation. God said to go possess the land, and the Israelites said, "We will send men before us, and they shall search out the land, and bring us word again by what way we must go up." Israel was saying that they would send out 12 spies to see if they were capable of possessing the land. Verse 23 says, "And the saying pleased me well…" because the idea to send the spies was not Moses' but God's (See Nu. 13:1-2). God said to go, and that is exactly what He wanted Israel to do. God was displeased with Israel's decision to listen to the spies who came back with a negative report.

It was the Israelites' unbelief that caused them to fear, when searching out the land God said to possess. There was not reason for them to fear when they sent the spies to observe the situation. God knew the way they should go, and He would have led them by the same means He led them from Egypt, a cloud by day and a pillar of fire by night. Israel did not have to measure the strength of their enemies. They weren't able to deliver themselves from the Egyptians. Their deliverance came from the power of God. If they would obey God's command, and go in and possess the land, He would deliver their enemies into their hands. Unbelief was the force that caused Israel to do what seemed right in their own eyes.

The writer of Hebrews tells us in Hebrews 3:12 that unbelief stems from an evil heart, and we are to take heed unless it controls of our lives and causes us to fail in obeying God's Word. What we don't realize is that when Christians permit unbelief to control our thoughts, they are choosing to take sides against the Word of God. When we take sides against God's Word, we limit the benefits Jesus has provided for us through Calvary. But when we, by faith, respond to God's Word and possess what is rightfully ours, our faith sets off a two-fold reaction!

- God ministers on our behalf to meet our needs, and
- Our lives change and become pleasing to God.

Paul tells us in Hebrews 11:6,

> *"But without faith it is impossible to please Him: For he that comes to God must believe that He is, and He is a rewarder of them that diligently seek Him"*

If it is impossible to please God without faith, the opposite of that truth is that with faith we are pleasing to God.

Another important fact Christians need always remember is when God speaks to us in His Word, there is no neutrality.

We either act upon God's Word by faith and enjoy the benefits of our obedience, or we refuse to act upon His Word because of our unbelief and suffer the consequences. There is one sure indication that unbelief is taking hold of our lives. If after reading God's Word pertaining to a subject we consult with other Christians, so as to obtain their opinion on the subject, before we act upon the Word of God. Remember that public opinion isn't always correct. It was public opinion that decided to crucify Christ. Public opinion often is swayed by so called facts, not faith. Walking with God oftentimes goes against facts, but instead determines unwaveringly to stand on God's Word by faith. Faith knows if God said it in His Word, no matter what the facts may state, God's Word will prevail!

Hezekiah's Stand

The Bible provides a wonderful illustration of this truth in Isaiah 36-38. King Sennacherib of Assyria and his armies came against King Hezekiah of Judah to take them captive. King Sennacherib sent a message to King Hezekiah and told him that his armies had Jerusalem surrounded, and that they might as well surrender because they didn't have a chance to escape or to defeat them. To add more facts in his favor, King Sennacherib reminded King Hezekiah that he was outnumbered, and the Assyrians had defeated every other country around them. This pointed to the fact that no other nation would come to the aid or rescue of Hezekiah.

Sennacherib also told Hezekiah that they should not deceive themselves into thinking that their God was going to help them defeat them. None of the gods of the neighboring countries were able to assist them in defeating the Assyrian army. Even though all of these facts clearly painted a picture of certain defeat, Hezekiah refused to believe his adversary. Instead, he stood against them by placing his faith in the delivering power of Almighty God.

King Hezekiah sought God in prayer, and God told him not to be afraid of the Assyrian army, for He would defeat them. That night God sent the death angel into the Assyrian camp and 185,000 Assyrians were killed and Judah was spared from certain defeat. So often, as it was in this story, facts spell out defeat, but faith in God's Word will provide us with the victory we need.

Another sure warning that unbelief is operating in one's life is when one tells God, "I'll obey your Word if you show me a special sign." When Christians talk in this manner, they are really testing God. First of all, you don't need a sign to obey what God has already told you. Secondly, the Bible never tells us to seek signs as a means to increase our faith or to act upon God's Word. God's Word doesn't tell us that faith follows signs, but rather signs follow faith.

When Israel sent out the spies, they returned with a thorough report. Their report stated that the land was good. It was everything that God said it would be, but they said,

> *"We can't possess it". "The cities have treat walls, and the people are giants. If we go against them, we will be defeated."*

Their report was one-hundred percent right. They couldn't possess the land in their own might or power. But they forgot that they weren't facing the enemies of the land alone, but they would possess the land by the might and power of God, if they obeyed His Word.

When the Israelites heard the report of the spies, they murmured and complained against God, refusing to obey

His Word. Their excuse for not possessing their complete redemption is summarized in Deuteronomy 1:28,

> *"Whither shall we go up? Our brethren have discouraged our heart..."*

How foolish for the people, who saw God manifest Himself on their behalf in Egypt, and at the crossing of the Red Sea, to believe such a discouraging report instead of believing God's command to them.

Christians today look back at Israel's lack of faith and are smugly critical of them. Yet, how many Christians today are just as guilty as the Israelites of the past? God has spoken to us in His Word, relating to us what Christ has provided for us through the atonement. Many Christians lack faith in God's Word because they fail to possess what is rightfully theirs. It is time or Christians to hear God speaking to them through His Word, believing it so that they can go forth and possess what is rightfully theirs.

The children of Israel became discouraged and disobeyed God's Word when they listened to the report of the ten spies. These ten spies were filled with unbelief, because they looked at the circumstances instead of the God who would give them victory over the circumstances. Christians must learn to look at the Word of God for direction, instead of to other Christians alone.[2] So many Christians are filled with unbelief and doubt. If we would look to them for encouragement to act upon God's Word, they might only damper our faith with their doubt.

---

[2] Of course, seeking wise counsel is commended by God, but the wisest of counsel must be rejected if contrary to God's Word.

Thank God for Joshua and Caleb. Even though they were outnumbered 10 to 2 (in terms of the spies), they came back with a good report saying,

> *"Let us go up and possess the land".*

Because they were willing to believe God instead of circumstances, they were the only two Israelite men over twenty years of age to possess and enjoy their full inheritance.

Ten spies saw giants in the land. Joshua and Caleb saw God. Joshua and Caleb had supernatural vision. They didn't see things merely through their natural eyes, but they saw through the eye of faith. That is exactly what Christians need today. Instead of seeing defeat, we need to see God working for us and granting us all that we need when we need it. What is needed today in the lives of Christians is an eye transplant from our natural vision to the supernatural vision of God. When we commit our lives to God by faith, we are no longer a natural creation, but we become a new creation born of the Spirit of God, which is a supernatural act. When we have supernatural sight and begin to walk by faith, we are going to see Christ moving in a supernatural way.
The Bible repeats in Deuteronomy 2:1 Israel's' tragic defeat. A defeat they experienced because they failed to accept by faith all that God had provided for them.

> *"Then we turned, and took our journey into the wilderness by the way of the Red Sea, as the Lord spake unto me: and we compassed Mount Seir many days."*

Instead of turning back into the wilderness, Israel would have been walking on Canaan's ground, possessing their inheritance, if it hadn't been for their unbelief.

Christian friend, will your experience be as Israel's? Will you continue around the mountain of your experience? Will you suffer defeat when Christ has provided you with complete redemption? Will you enjoy the fullness of your salvation? The very force that will determine whether we are defeated or we possess our inheritance is our faith in God's Word. If we believe in His Word, and act upon it, we will enjoy a rich, fulfilling life. But if unbelief takes hold of our lives, life will never be what it should be. We will exist and not really live. It is up to us to decide whether we will believe God's Word and act upon it, or doubt His word and suffer the consequences of our faithlessness. The soundest advice is what God advised Israel,

> *"Dread not, neither be afraid, for I will go with you and fight for you as I did for you in Egypt."*

If we are willing to possess our complete redemption by obeying God's Word by faith, God will defeat any obstacle Satan will put against us. Paul, knowing this, said it so profoundly in Romans 8:31,

> *"If God be for us, who can be against us?"*

Christian, go forth, possess your inheritance!

"Do you not know that those who run in a race all run, but only one receives the prize? Run in such a way that you may win." I Corinthians 9:24

Chapter V

What is Complete Redemption?

In previous chapters I have discussed quite extensively about our complete redemption. In this chapter, I want to share with you what complete redemption details. Christians have been guilty of defining complete redemption as salvation, yet this is not fully true. You can be saved, on your way to heaven, and still not enjoy all the benefits Christ has provided for you through Calvary's cross. Salvation is a most important part of complete redemption. As a matter of fact, it is the foundation, but salvation is not the end of the story, but the beginning.

Paul, in Ephesians 1:3, best defines complete redemption.

> *"Blessed be the God and Father of our Lord Jesus Christ, who has blessed us with all spiritual blessings in heavenly places in Christ."*

Paul states that complete redemption is being blessed with all the benefits Christ provided for us in the atonement. Don't be deceived into thinking that these benefits are only for our spiritual needs, because Paul calls them, "spiritual" blessings. The atonement is Christ's provision for the whole man; his physical, emotional and spiritual needs. Paul calls these benefits "spiritual blessings" because Jesus is the one who has provided them for us.

Throughout Jesus' earthly ministry, the Bible portrays His concern for every aspect of man's life. In the sixth chapter of Mark, Jesus and His disciples went to a desert place to get rest. When the people saw Jesus leave, they followed after Him. When Jesus saw this, the Bible says,

> *"And He was moved with compassion towards them, because they were as sheep not having a shepherd, and He began to teach them many things."*

Jesus loved these people and recognized that they had a spiritual need, so He proceeded to meet that need.

One important truth Jesus projects in this passage is that love is more than just being concerned about a need. Love reacts to the need by meeting the need. After Jesus had ministered all day to the people's spiritual needs, Mark points out another amazing truth. Jesus was also concerned about their physical need. The day was far spent, evening was coming and the people hadn't eaten any natural food all day. The disciples said to Jesus,

> *"Send them away, that they may to into the country round about and into the villages, and buy themselves bread." (Mark 6:36)*

Jesus told His disciples to feed them. You can imagine the disciple's expressions when Jesus gave them this command. There must have been expressions of shock, perplexity, and doubt. They told Jesus that they could not fulfill His request because they didn't have enough food to feed the multitude of people. Jesus asked them what they had. All they could find among the people were five loaves of bread and two fish. That certainly wasn't enough food to feed five thousand people (plus women and children). Jesus thought it was enough and told them to organize the people in groups of hundreds and fifties. Jesus took the elements He had, and proceeded to feed every one of the five thousand plus people. Why? Because Jesus was concerned about the needs of the people He loved.

In other passages of Scripture Jesus healed lepers, opened the eyes of the blind, or healed people of all types of sickness during His earthly ministry. He was concerned with man's physical need.

The Word of God also tells us that Christ is concerned with His children's financial needs (one of the key concerns of the soul). He tells us in His Word not to worry about financial needs. In Matthew 6:25, 26 we are told,

> *"For this reason I say to you, do not be anxious for your life, as to what you shall eat, or what ye shall drink; nor for your body, as to what you shall put on. Look at the birds of the air; that they do not sow, neither do they reap, nor gather into barns, and yet your heavenly Father feeds them. Are you not worth much more than they?"*

A final picture of the Lord's care is seen in Philippians 4:19, where Paul tells us as God's children we don't have to worry about our financial needs because

> *"My God shall supply all your need according to His riches in glory by Christ Jesus."*

Of course, this was predicated on generous giving, first giving ones heart then finances for the support of the work of God.

Many times in my own life I have found that when all my financial resources have been exhausted, and I needed money for groceries or to pay a bill, God supplied the need through an unexpected source. Jesus, while here on earth, was concerned about every man's need. That is why He ministered to the needs of everyone who came to Him.

His love for man provides the very reason there was a Calvary's Cross. It was at Calvary that Jesus, through His death and resurrection, paid the price for our full redemption. In doing so, Jesus provides to every human being in every generation the opportunity to come to Him, permitting Him to minister to every type of need.

As we examine Jesus' dying words, we will note they were definite and positive. As He was about to die, He made a proclamation to all mankind. In the eyes of the people surrounding Golgotha's hill it looked as though Jesus' life was wasted. Many of the people had thought (correctly, but incompletely) He was the Messiah, the Deliverer of Israel. But as He was hanging on the cross, He looked more like a common thief. What possible meaning could these final words have that were uttered by such a disgraced man? Little did they know that the words Jesus was about to proclaim would be the declaration of reconciliation between God and man.

It is Finished

Jesus' proclamation was "It was finished." What was finished? The provision for man's complete redemption. Through His death, Jesus satisfied God's price of redemption. Man no longer need be alienated from God. From then until now, all men, by faith in the broken body and shed blood of Jesus Christ, have the power to become the sons and daughters of God.

John tells us this in John 1:12,

> *"But as many as received Him, to them gave He power to become the children of God, even to them that believe on His name."*

We no longer need to live under the penalty of death for our sins. Jesus became our substitute, paying our debt at Calvary. We can possess life eternal by accepting His payment of our sins by faith in Him. Paul states in Romans 6:23,

> *"The wages of sin is death, but the gift of God is eternal life through Jesus Christ our Lord."*

Freedom from Sin

Complete redemption goes beyond providing forgiveness for our past sins. It also includes Christ's work in keeping us from living in sin. So often Christians fail to realize this important truth, because they make excuses for living in sin. Paul, in Romans 13:14 reminds Christians not to make provisions or excuses for living in sin.

> *"But put on the Lord Jesus Christ, and make no provision for the flesh in regards to its lusts."*

Yet you still hear Christians saying, "I have to sin daily because I'm just human. If I was perfect, God would take me out of this world to be with Him in Heaven." That excuse is nothing but a lie from the pit of Hell. Christ the Savior has come to live within us. He is perfect and He wills for Christians to be like Him. Jesus tells us in Matthew 5:48,

> "Therefore, you are to be perfect, as your heavenly Father is perfect."

If Jesus didn't think we could be perfect[3], he would never have told us in His Word to be perfect. God is just and He never would demand us to be or do something He knew we could not be or do.

The reason why Christians yield to sin and fail to overcome it that they have failed to recognize Christ lives in them. Paul, in Galatians 2:20, reminds Christians of this glorious fact.

> *"I am crucified with Christ; nevertheless, I live; yet not I, but Christ lives in me; and the life I now live in the flesh, I live by the faith of the Son of God, who loved me, and gave Himself for me."*

In essence, Paul was saying, "I can be what God wills me to be, because I have surrendered my life to Christ and I permit Him to live trough me." When we permit Christ to live through us, He will lead and guide us in the daily decisions we make. He will strengthen us to overcome temptations instead of yielding to sin. When we overcome sin, instead of being tormented by it, we enjoy the blessing of the overcomer. John, in Revelation chapters two or three, outlines the blessings Christ has promised Christians who are overcomers.

I urge Christians to realize this important fact; Christ lives in you. Since He lives in you, decide from this moment on that you are going to permit Him to reign and control your

---

[3] (That is, fully mature, separated unto God for his purpose, able to resist sin and having the desire to do so.)

life, giving you power to live an overcoming life. Always remember this, you can't live an overcoming life in your own strength and power. John says it so adequately in 1 John 4:4.

> *"You are from God, little children, and have overcome them; because greater is He who is in you, than He who is in the world."*

Christ in us will supersede every temptation that may come against us.

Holy Spirit

Complete redemption also includes the Baptism in the Holy Spirit. God always intended that the Baptism of the Holy Spirit be a part of our redemption.[4] Man has been guilty of trying to segregate it to just the Age of the Apostles, but we find out differently in Acts 2:38, 39.

> *"...and you shall receive the gift of the Holy Spirit. For the promise is unto you, and to your children, and to all that are afar off, even as many as the Lord, our God, shall call."*

In the Old Testament, God revealed to the prophet Joel that in the last days (the days of complete redemption after Calvary), He would pour out His Spirit upon all flesh. Peter, on the day of Pentecost, after the 120 received the Baptism of the Holy Spirit, stated,

---

[4] Of course, we are saved (regenerated) by the Holy Spirit, so all believers have the Spirit. The Baptism of the Holy Spirit speaks of receiving His fullness, or if you will, allowing the Holy Spirit (God) to have all of us.

> *"This is that which was spoken through the prophet Joel." (Acts 2:16)*

John the Baptist prophesied the coming of the Holy Spirit when he baptized Jesus in water. Matthew 3:11 says,

> *"He (Jesus) shall baptize you with the Holy Spirit, and with fire."*

John's prophesy was fulfilled after Calvary. After Jesus ascended into heaven, He poured out the Holy Spirit upon His followers and also to every believer who has desired it since then.

Jesus, in John 16:7, prophesied on the coming of the Baptism of the Holy Spirit. He said,

> *"It is expedient for you (a better translation is 'it is better for you') that I go away, for if I go not away, the Comforter (which is the Holy Spirit) will not come unto you; but if I depart, I will send him unto you."*

Jesus also told His disciples before He ascended to heaven in Acts 1:8,

> *"But you shall receive power, after the Holy Spirit is come upon you; and you shall be witnesses unto me both in Jerusalem, and in all Judah, and in Samaria, and unto the uttermost part of the earth."*

Jesus has provided us with the Baptism of the Holy Spirit to lead and guide us into all truth. The Holy Spirit also empowers us to be a witness for Him. Jesus wasn't talking about an ordinary witness, but a special kind; a witness

with signs and wonders following the teaching of His Word.
Jesus has also provided us with the Baptism of the Holy Spirit so we can enjoy answers to prayer. Paul points this truth out to us in 1 Corinthians 14:2, 14,

> *"For one who speaks in a tongue does not speak to men, but to God: for no man understands; but in his spirit he speaks mysteries." "For if I pray in a tongue, my spirit prays, but my mind is unfruitful."*

When we pray in an unknown tongue, we are not talking to man, we are communicating with God on His frequency. He understands what we are saying.

Many times when we pray concerning a need, we don't know how to pray. Our understanding is limited and our vocabulary cannot express the right words. When we pray in tongues, the Holy Spirit speaks through us and we see God answering our prayers.

Every Christian needs the Baptism of the Holy Spirit, because it is part of our complete redemption that Christ has provided for us. Jesus said in Mark 16:17-18 that the Baptism of the Holy Spirit doesn't save us, but is another confirmation that we are believers.

> *"And these signs shall follow those who believe..." "They shall speak with new tongues, they shall take up serpents; and if they drink any deadly thing, it shall not hurt them; they shall lay lands on the sick, and they shall recover."*

It is time for us as believers to possess our full inheritance and receive the fullness of the Holy Spirit. How can you receive the Baptism of the Holy Spirit? By believing God wants you to have it, as we have just pointed out. Then, we are to ask God to give it to us. Once you ask God for it, then you are to thank God for giving it to you. As you are thanking God for giving it to you, He will release the words you will say, and as you speak these words in faith, you are possessing or receiving the fullness of Holy Spirit.

Gifts

Complete redemption does not end with the Baptism of the Holy Spirit. It also includes a manifestation of the gifts of the Spirit. Paul, in 1 Corinthians 12:8-10, lists nine gifts of the Spirit. Before Paul listed the gifts, he wrote,

> *"But to each one is given the manifestation of the Spirit for the common good."*

In other words, Paul is telling Christians the manifestation of these gifts can be exercised by any believer, for the good of other believers.

Each Christian can and should manifest the gifts of the Spirit or any aspect of their redemption by following the principle God has given us in Matthew 21:22.

> *"And all things, whatever you ask in prayer believing, you shall receive."*

In order for us the manifest the gifts of the Spirit, we need to ask God for them in prayer. Once we ask God for them, we need to believe He will give them to us. His Word states that it is His will to give us what we ask, so all we need to do is receive from Him. We receive them by obeying the voice of the Holy Spirit and using the gift that is needed in whatever situation confronts us.

In one of my meetings, a young man who had just received the Baptism of the Holy Spirit asked me to pray for him to receive the gift of tongues and interpretation. We prayed and asked God to give him these gifts. Then I asked him if He believed God answered our prayer. He said he did. Later in the meeting, a brother gave a message in tongues. For awhile there was no interpretation. Finally, I gave the interpretation. After the service the young man came to me and told me the Holy Spirit had given him the same interpretation I had given, but he didn't speak out because he thought is was just his imagination.
We can ask God to give us a certain gift of the Sprit and He will. However, in order to receive the gift, we must obey the leadership of the Holy Spirit and use the gift that has been given to us when the occasion calls for it.

Christ has made these gifts available to each Christian for the edification of the Body of Christ, which is His church. The reason our churches today are spiritually dying while the occult, astrology and Satan worship are growing, is that Christians are neglecting the use of the gifts of the Spirit. We have tried to convert the world with our programs, which are often only a form of godliness, but lacking in the real power of the Spirit.

Jesus has provided the church with the means to strength itself. We must take advantage of His provision, and possess the gifts of the Spirit made readily available to us by the Spirit.

If Christianity is going to be revitalized once again, we need the word of wisdom, the word of knowledge, faith, the gifts of healing, the working of miracles, prophecy, discerning of spirits, and tongues and interpretation in operation in our assemblies.

Healing

Another blessing Christ has provided us as part of our complete redemption is healing. As stated earlier in this chapter, when a person comes to Jesus in His earthly ministry for healing, He heals them. When a leper came to Him in Luke 5:12 and asked Jesus if He willed to heal him, Jesus said,

> *"I will, be clean. And immediately the leprosy departed from him."*

How often Christians quote Hebrews 13:8,

> *"Jesus Christ the same yesterday, and today, and forever."*

I doubt whether the majority of Christians truly believe what they are saying. When sickness comes, they immediately accept it, and make preparations to live with their illness. They run to the best doctors, take the best pills, and proclaim to the world, "It is God's will for me to be sick." The only time they really start praying for their healing is when the doctor says, "We have done everything medical science can do for you. There isn't anything else we can do."

If we really believe that Jesus Christ is the same yesterday, today, and forever, then when sickness comes, instead of making preparation to live with our sickness, we will come to Jesus by faith, knowing He wills to heal us because healing is part of our redemption. We will push through the doubts and pain, and touch the hem of His garment in prayer, and here Jesus say, "Thy faith has made you whole."

Where did sickness get its origin? In Deuteronomy 28 we are told that sickness stems from the curse of the law or sin. If there wasn't sin in this world, there wouldn't be sickness. God told Israel that if they obeyed His Word, He would protect them from sickness. If they failed to obey, then He would allow Satan to attack their bodies with sickness.

I am not saying that if you are suffering sickness today it is because you have disobeyed God's Word. Although, if you harbor bitterness, jealousy, hatred, or any other sin in your heart, you are disobeying God's Word, and you are leaving yourself open for any sickness Satan wants to attack you with.

Satan has also attacked righteous men and women when God has permitted him to do so in the past. A good example of this is found in Job. He suffered with boils all over his body, though God called him perfect. We also note that Job was trusting God for his deliverance, and the Bible says that God did heal him.

Paul, in Galatians 3:13, tells us that Jesus Christ paid the price for us at Calvary's cross, and has redeemed us from the curse of the law. He paid for our sins and our sickness. In order for us to enjoy such a redemption, we are to play an important part. We must accept His provision for our sickness by faith. You may say, "How can I accept healing by faith?" First of all, we have to know what God's Word says about healing. Do you have a right to be healed? Or is healing just for a segregated few?

Jesus in His Word says in Matthew 11:28,

> *"Come unto me, all you that labor and are heavy laden, and I will give you rest."*

If you are sick, you have a heavy burden and need rest or healing from your sickness. Jesus is telling you that if you want healing you must "Come unto Me, ask Me for it, believe that I will do it, then receive it by thanking Me for your healing."

Jesus said in Matthew 21:22,

> *"And all things, whatsoever you ask in prayer, believing, you shall receive."*

Is that verse true or false? Did Jesus really mean what He said? If that verse is false, then everything else in the Bible is false. If Jesus told one lie, then He was a sinner and needed someone to die for Him. One thing we must realize is that Jesus always meant what He said. Man is the one who is guilty of trying to change the meaning of God's Word. Man likes to put words into God's Word, which usually causes confusion.

The Bible tells us why Jesus wills to heal us. Jesus bore our sickness upon His body on Calvary's cross. The prophet Isaiah prophesied years before Calvary about Jesus bearing our sicknesses for us when he wrote in Chapter 53:5,

> *"But He was wounded for our transgressions, He was bruised for our iniquities; the punishment for our peace was upon Him, and with His stripes we are healed."*

Matthew reaffirms Isaiah's words about Jesus in chapter 8, verses 16 and 17,

> *"When the evening was come, they brought to Him many that were possessed with demons; and He cast out the spirits with His word and healed* ***all*** *that were sick, that it might be fulfilled which was spoken by Isaiah, the prophet, saying that He himself took our infirmities, and bore our sicknesses."*

The apostle Peter, years after Calvary, looks back to the cross and its provisions and writes in I Peter 2:24,

> *"...by whose stripes ye were healed."*

Of course, "were" denotes past tense. Our healing was provided for us 2,000 years ago on Calvary's cross.

Now that we know from God's Word that healing is part of our redemption, we must possess it by faith. You may say, What if I asked God to heal me and I don't feel healed? Am I healed?" What is the proof of your healing, your feelings or God's Word? God's Word is the proof. If you have asked God in the name of Jesus for your healing, and you believe He has heard your prayer, continue to thank God for your healing, no matter how you feel. You are not lying or being a hypocrite. You are possessing that which belongs to you. By faith you will be rewarded with the fact of your healing.

After we receive Christ as our Savior, we don't necessarily feel saved, yet that doesn't mean we are not saved. If we have confessed our sins to Christ and believe He has forgiven us, He has, because He said He would in His

Word. If we have asked God to heal us, no matter how you may feel, thank God for healing you, because He tells us in His Word, "by His stripes you were healed." I urge you who are sick in body to possess your physical healing right now, because it belongs to you.

Many of you may not by physically sick, but you need a mental or emotional healing. You may suffer from depression where there isn't a logical reason for it. Sometimes it can be something that has happened in the past that your subconscious mind is remembering. The Lord can heal those unpleasant memories and give you peace. God has provided healing for your body, mind, and soul. You must contend for it by faith. It's part of your redemption.

Prosperity

Prosperity, or financial blessing, is part of the fruit of our life in Christ. Much has been written on this subject, from the ridiculous (if you are not rich, you are not spiritual) to the sublime (prosperity is a gift from the Lord to fulfill the covenant of God, see Deut. 8:18).

I believe in prosperity because I'm going somewhere

Perhaps the most quoted (and misquoted) passage of scripture on prosperity is found in III John 2. John states,

> *"Beloved, I pray that in all respects you may prosper and be in health, just as your soul prospers."*

In the original language, the word prosper (euodoo) means "to help on the road, succeed in reaching, to succeed in business affairs, to have a prosperous journey" In fact if you are not going anywhere, have no purpose goals or vision you need very little. But if you are going somewhere in God, have a family to care for, a ministry to serve, a purpose to fulfill, you can trust that the Lord will indeed prosper you, providing all you need for life's journey. Trust Him for it, believe God's word, and you will see the might provision of the Lord for your life.

CONCLUSION

It is time that God's precious saints begin to live the abundant life Jesus promised us. One the one hand, as Paul stated, we have already received all blessings in Christ. (Eph 1:3). Yet in this life, the blessings we have received by promise in Christ are to be manifested in the Kingdom of God on earth, through the lives of His saints. My prayer for you echoes John's

> *"...I would that in all things you might prosper and be in healthy",*

and Paul's in I Thes. 5:23…

> *"Now may the God of peace Himself sanctify you entirely; and may your spirit and soul and body be preserved complete, without blame at the coming of our Lord Jesus Christ" Amen!*

About the Author

Dr. Anthony Spero began his ministry, along with his wife Mary, as an evangelist shortly after completing his Diploma of Theology from Zion Bible Institute in Providence, Rhode Island. After a prosperous time on the road, Dr. Spero settled into a pastorate in Fairmont, West Virginia for five years. For the next 2 and half years he held evangelistic services in different parts of the United States. Then for 25 years he pastored Calvary Chapel Christian Center in Severn, Maryland. During his time at Calvary, he also fathered two other churches in the state of Maryland and several churches on the continent of Africa. During his time of pastoring in Maryland he also began a successful Christian Academy and Bible College, and developed a network for Pastor's prayer for the greater Baltimore area. The church grew and prospered under his leadership, but not without struggle and hard work.

Dr. Spero has always had a heart for training national leaders for effective ministry in the nations. He has demonstrated his love for the nations by traveling and ministering to the nations of the world. In the late nineties, Dr. Spero and his partner in ministry, Mary felt the strong leading of the Lord that their time in Maryland was over. He was offered the opportunity to be a part of planting a new church in Fort Myers, Florida and to become the Dean of the Faith International Training School, a ministry outreach of Faith Fellowship Ministries World Outreach Center lead by Dr. David T. Demola. This continues as the key assignment of the Spero's life. This school is a six-month intensive training course for national and international pastors and church leaders.

As dean, teacher and spiritual enrichment pastor of F.I.T.S. Dr. Spero is able to impart 40 years of spiritual leadership that has been imparted to him into national and international leaders, while continuing to teach and demonstrate a life of faith in conferences and through international outreach.

Finally, Dr. Spero is the proud husband of one (Mary), father of two beautiful daughters, Pamela and Lisa, inheritor of two sons-in-law, Charles and Monty, and the very proud 'poppi' (grandfather) of Kayla, Christopher and Noah. Dr. Spero can be reached for special speaking engagements and faith inspiring teaching at:

Faith International Training School
6111 South Pointe Blvd.
Fort. Myers, Florida 33919

Other Material by Dr. Anthony Spero

Book

"The Gospel Jesus Lived and Preached"

Tapes Series

Your a Winner
Arrow in God's Quiver
Victory Over Difficulties
Going The Distance
Now Is Your Time
You Have A Future
Experiencing God's Promises

For more information on life changing books published by Vision Publishing, see the list below and view all our books at www.visionpublishingservices.com and for information on studying with Vision International College and University see us at www.vision.edu

Books by Dr. Ken Chant

- **Faith Dynamics: Studies in Faith**
- **Mountain Movers: More Studies on Faith**
- **Christian Life: Patterns of Gracious Living**
- **Equipped to Serve: (subtitle)**
- **Healing in the Whole Bible**
- **The Cross and the Crown: Studies in our Great Salvation**

Books by Dr. Stan DeKoven

- **Fresh Manna: How to Study the Word**
- **New Beginnings: Our First Steps in Christ**
- **40 Days to the Promise: A Way through the Wilderness**
- **Journey of the Kingdom: Becoming Whole in Christ**
- **Supernatural Architecture: Preparing the Church of the 21st Century**
- **I Want to Be Like You, Dad: Breaking Generational Patterns and Restoring the Fathers Heart**

Books by other Vision authors

- **Fruit, More Fruit, Much Fruit: A Study on the Fruit of the Holy Spirit by Dr. Eugene Smith**
- **Bringing Heaven to Earth: Fulfilling the Great Commission by Dr. Timothy Dailey**

Printed in the United States
49512LVS00002B/16-66